EXOTIC
Tillandsia
II

SIM ENG HIANG, FRPS

Copyright © 2017 Sim Eng Hiang. All rights reserved.

ISBN
978-1-4828-8270-4 (sc)
978-1-4828-8271-1 (e)

All rights reserved. No part of this book may be used or reproduced by any means, graphic, electronic, or mechanical, including photocopying, recording, taping or by any information storage retrieval system without the written permission of the publisher except in the case of brief quotations embodied in critical articles and reviews.

Because of the dynamic nature of the Internet, any web addresses or links contained in this book may have changed since publication and may no longer be valid. The views expressed in this work are solely those of the author and do not necessarily reflect the views of the publisher, and the publisher hereby disclaims any responsibility for them.

Print information available on the last page.

To order additional copies of this book, contact
Toll Free 800 101 2657 (Singapore)
Toll Free 1 800 81 7340 (Malaysia)
www.partridgepublishing.com/singapore
orders.singapore@partridgepublishing.com

01/30/2017

PARTRIDGE

Dedicated to my Father

Sim Soo Khoon

And to the memory of my Mother

Tan Cho Siang

ACKNOWLEDGEMENTS

My father was a simple man. Each day he would ride his bicycle to work at dawn and return home late at night. He worked very hard to earn a living for his family of nine. He loved keeping plants and animals, and when I was a young boy I would help him take care of them. Years later I would take a keen interest in gardening.

These days almost everybody takes photographs, unlike in the '60s where few people owned cameras and photography was considered an expensive and luxurious hobby. One day my father brought home a camera to record certain events in our lives. No one in the family then knew how to use it, so being the eldest child I took up the challenge and spent what little money I had to learn how to take good pictures.

Here I must sincerely thank the late Mr. K.F. Wong, Honorary Fellow of the Royal Photographic Society, FRPS, who achieved world fame through his lifetime work with his subject, the indigenous peoples of Sarawak. He was someone who guided me and gave me much guidance and encouragement. I also want to thank a master of flower arrangement, Madame Chiou Yu-Chien, of Taiwan, who taught me the art of flower arrangement.

After all these years, gardening and photography still fill me with enthusiasm, and few things give me more joy than growing Tillandsia and photographing this beautiful creation of Mother Nature.

PREFACE

The two essences of life are health and happiness, and happiness to me is simplicity in life.

I consider myself fortunate to have picked gardening and photography as my hobbies. I started my gardening hobby by growing many different types of plants, until one day I was introduced by a friend to the exotic *Tillandsia*. I was immediately fascinated by this weird genus of plants, and by how a plant could grow without soil, even without roots. I then started collecting them. Now my garden is filled with the splendour of the many varieties of *Tillandsia*.

Because I nurture and grow *Tillandsia*, I was also able to capture them on camera when they were at their most beautiful. I have the pleasure of recording these moments each day, and have taken thousands of photographs. All the pictures were taken under natural lighting.

I am happy to be able to share with you some of the images I have taken over the years of this exotic genus. I hope this book will engage you to learn more about this wonderful gift from Mother Nature, the *Tillandsia*.

Let us not forget that plants give us life, and that without plants, all creatures would not survive. Let us cherish and protect our planet, our water, our air, and our plants.

INTRODUCTION

The *Tillandsia*, commonly known as the air plant, is the largest genus of the bromeliad family. It is found mainly in Latin America. *Tillandsia* grow on trees, rocks, cliffs, and on some types of cacti. They are epiphytes, not parasites.

They do not grow in soil, except for the popular house plant *Tillandsia cyanea*. The most attractive feature of *Tillandsia* is their ability to receive water and nutrients through the white fuzzy scales on their leaves called trichomes. Nutrients in the wild are provided by dust, decaying leaves, and insect matter. The wire-like roots have no root hairs and are only used to anchor the plant to a host. The plants can grow without roots and soil. This allows the grower almost unlimited freedom in creative decoration with live plants. Presentation is the key with these plants, in terms of their individual mounting and overall display. Your imagination is the only limit. One important fact is that *Tillandsia* are not toxic to animals. They can be glued, wired, or tied to just about anything, and they will flourish if given supportive growth conditions. Be aware, however, that plants that are stuck into holes often rot when their bases become wet and do not have the opportunity to dry out.

Most *Tillandsia*, with a few exceptions, bloom only once in the lifetime. When a plant reaches maturity, it blooms, with spikes that last from several weeks to many months. During and after blooming, new plants form at the plant's base or along the stem. Watching these small plants grow without soil is the real satisfaction in growing *Tillandsia*, and the blooms are the final reward. Plants grown from seed grow slowly and take a few years to mature.

Tillandsia are easy to grow; air, water, and light are all they need.

LIGHT

Tillandsia will tolerate bright, indirect light, including fluorescent office lighting. *Tillandsia* put indoors should receive plenty of light from a nearby window. If a full-spectrum fluorescent light that provides 92 percent of actual sunlight is used, it should be placed no further than 36 inches (90 cm) from the tube and can be as closed as 6 inches (15 cm) above the plants for 12 hours a day.

WATER

Thoroughly wet the plants two to three times a week – more often in a hot, dry environment and less often in cool, humid surroundings. When possible, totally submerge the plants once a month for ten minutes to several hours, depending on the condition of the plants. Then allow the base of the plant to dry before it is put back. If a plant is dehydrated, it is indicated by exaggerating the natural concave curve of the leaves. The appearance of the plants reveals its particular needs. Generally, plants with softer, green leaves require more moisture and prefer shaded areas. Plants with stiffer, silvery leaves require more light and less watering. They are usually from warmer areas. They should be allowed to dry out between watering. *Tillandsia* like slightly acidic water with a pH of about 6.0. Adding a little vinegar to the water will drop the pH.

AIR CIRCULATION

Tillandsia should be given enough light and air circulation to dry in four hours or less after watering. Do not keep plants constantly wet or moist. The optimum temperature range for *Tillandsia* is from 7°C to 35°C (45°F to 95°F). *Tillandsia* love fresh, moving air.

FERTILIZER

Water soluble foliar fertilizers can be used at 1/4 strength once a month. Water containing a diluted amount of fertilizer (a few drops in a litre of water) used every time the plants are watered is ideal.

Tillandsia duratii is one of the most successful Tillandsia speceies. It grows well under a wide range of light, water and temperature conditions. Without roots, the curly leaves cling to its host like a monkey. The inflorescene of Tillandsia duratii develops for several months, and produces lovely lavender flowers that are heavily fragrant.

Tillandsia Juncifolia. The plant is easy to grow and always grow in large clumps. It flourishes when mounted in any position.

Tillandsia funckiana is a lovely plant and easy to grow, frequently grow many offsets along the stem and form a magnificent clump. It grows well in an airy, bright location.

Tillandsia funckiana growing in a clump.

Tillandsia ionantha v. vanhyningii. There are many forms of Tillandsia ionantha. It is the only form of ionantha that is caulescent. It has thick, succulent leaves and slow growing. It comes from one cliff in Mexico and is relatively rare.

Tillandsia velutina. This plant comes from Guatemala. It has a velvety look and feel. It likes plenty of water and bright location.

Tillandsia rodrigueziana x Tillandsia brachycaulos. The leaves of this beautiful hybrid are apple green, softer and thinner than the T. rodrigueziana. It is very easy to grow.

Tillandsia rodrigueziana x *Tillandsia brachyculos growing on an old coconut.*

Tillandsia harrisii. This is a very attractive and extremely hardy species. The thick soft leaves have a velvety surface. The plant produces a single pinkish to red inflorescence with tubular purple flowers.

Bathing in the sunny rain. Tillandsias are found mainly in the tropical rainforest in the Latin America, so light, water and air circulation are the key factors for keeping healthy Tilladnsia.

Tillandsia bulbosa. A very attractive plant with long, twisting cylindrical bright-green leaves that grow from a bulbous base. When in bloom, it produces bracts that become bright red, from which emerge tubular purple flowers. It produces a few offsets around the base of the parent plant after flowering, and becoming a spectacular multi-plant specimen in time.

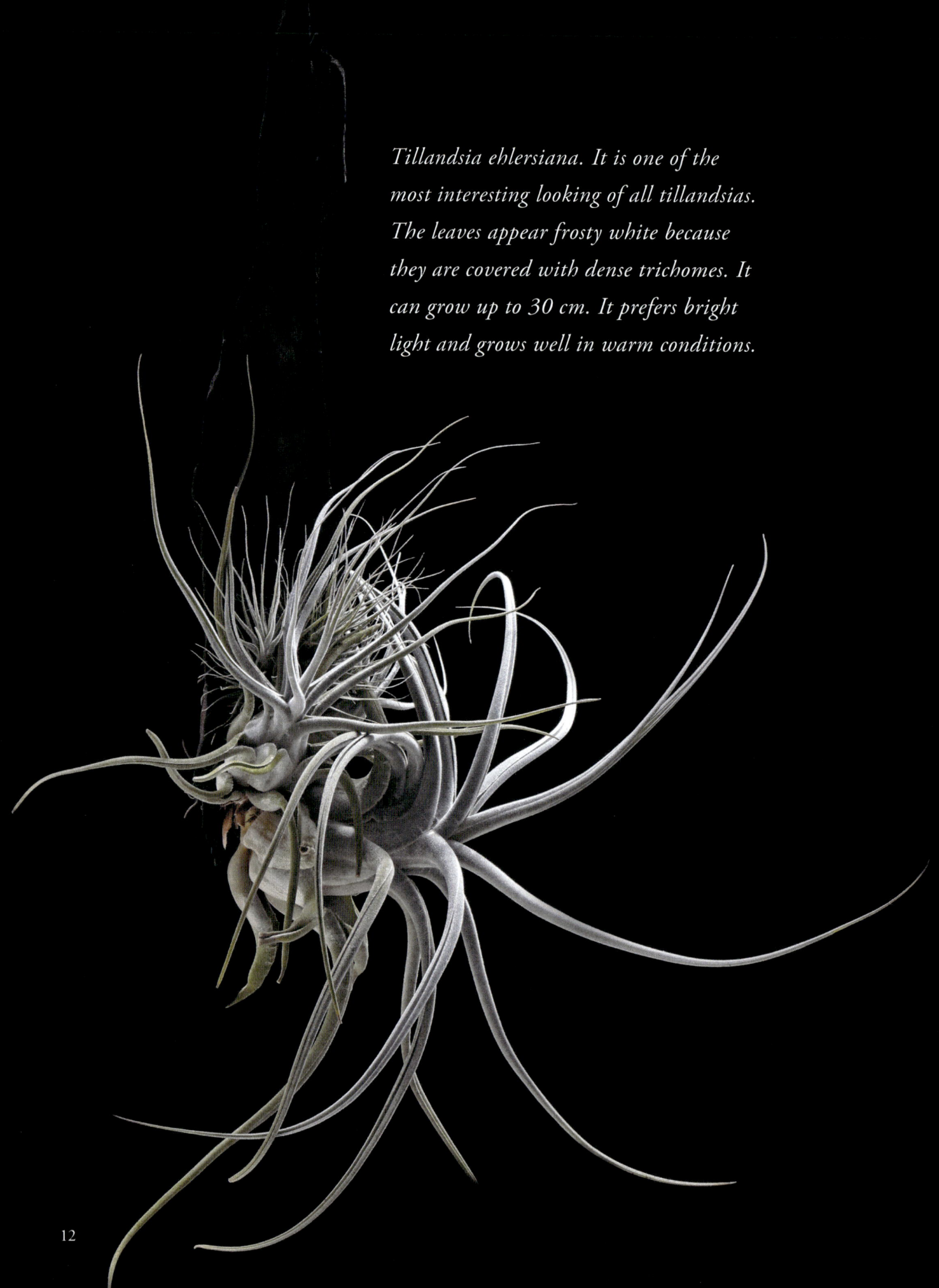

Tillandsia ehlersiana. It is one of the most interesting looking of all tillandsias. The leaves appear frosty white because they are covered with dense trichomes. It can grow up to 30 cm. It prefers bright light and grows well in warm conditions.

Tillandsia baileyi. It is a stemless species that always grow in dense clumps. It is easy to take care and can grow to quite large in good conditions.

Tillandsia funckiana x *Tillandsia ionantha*. This beautiful hybrid is easy to grow but slow growing.

Tillandsia pseudobaileyi. It has a frosted, silvery appearance as the plant is densely covered with trichomes. The leaves are furrowed longitudinally with thin amethyst lines. This does not appear on caput-medusae, baileyi, butzii and bulbosa. It is a slow growing plant and needs frequent watering.

A beautiful display of Tillandsia pseudobaiyi in the morning light.

Tillandsia filifolia is a popular species among collectors. The leaves are long, thin and green in colour, so it requires watering frequently in dry climates. It normally produces two or three offsets. Seedling grown from seeds needs some ten to twelve years to mature.

Tillandsia vernicosa. It is a hardy species, and the leaves are stiff and brittle. It looks very much like Tillandsia concolor but much smaller. The floral bracts are red and the flowers are white.

Tillandsia vernicosa.

Tillandsia recurvifolia v. subsecundifolia. It is a hardy plants that requires bright light to thrive. It looks like T. harrisii but the leaves are curve and grow to one side.

Tillandsia ionantha 'Fuego'. Tillandsia ionantha is a popular species and is always the first Tillandsia one acquires. It is attractive, small and easy to cultivate. The leaves always form a pretty rosette. It often grows in clumps. When in bloom, the leaves of most ionantha flush to red, with tubular purple flowers. There are many forms of Tillandsia ionantha. Plants from different areas have different forms, sizes, shapes and colors.

Tillandsia ionantha 'Rosita'.

Tillandsia ionantha 'Guat'.

A small form of Tillandsia ionantha.

A few forms of Tillandsia ionantha growing on a piece of drift wood.

A beautiful display of Tillandsia filifolia and Tillandsia ionantha growing together on a piece of drift wood.

The graceful form of Tillsndsia filifolia and the dwarf form of Tillandsia ionantha match perfectly.

Tillandsias can grow on trees, rocks and cliffs, not in soil. Without roots, they can also survive. So we can use them to create Tillandsia bonsai.

A small bonsai growing on a piece of rock.

Tillandsia bonsai.

Tillandsia bonsai.

Tillandsia bonsai.

A few species of Tillandsia growing on a jar to create this bonsai.

Landscape bonsai.

Tillandsia bonsai.

A few small plants growing on the stem of a tall plant.

Tillandsia bonsai.

Tillandsia bonsai.

Tillandsia bonsai.

Tillandsia bonsai.

Tillandsia bonsai.

Tillandsia bonsai.

Tillandsia bonsai.

Tillandsia bonsai.

Tillandsia bonsai.

Tillandsia bonsai.

Tillandsia bonsai.

Tillandsia fasciculata. Tillandsia fasciculata varies greatly in its natural habitat. They are easy to grow, They prefer bright light, fresh air and frequent watering. They grow well in open space. It often grows into a large specimen, and serves as the centerpiece of one's collection.

Tillandsia caput-medusae. It is one of the most widespread and hardy species. It is stemless and quite variable in size. The twisted, narrow, thick, channelled leaves grow from the bulbous body. A very popular plant and easy to grow.

Tillandsias caput-medusae purple.

Tillandsia caput-medusae.

Tillandsia brachycaulos 'Selecta". Brachycaulos is from the Greek 'brachy' meaning 'short', and 'caulos 'meaning 'stem'. It is a widespread species with a number of forms and easy to grow, best with strong light and sufficient watering. Tillandsia beachycaulos 'Selecta' has apple-green leaves that turn ruby red when in bloom.

Another form a fasiculata.

Tillandsia reichenbachii. It looks like a small Tillandsia duratii. It rarely grows more than 16 cm. across and 10 cm. tall. The flowers are fragrant and have three different colors, deep purple, light purple and white.

Tillandsia brachycaulos "Selecta. Brachycaulos is from the Greek brachy, meaning 'short', and caulos, meaning 'stem'. It id s widespread species with a number of forms. It is easy to grow, best with strong light and sufficient watering. Tillandsia brachycaulos 'Selecta' has apple-green leaves that turn ruby red when in bloom.

Tillandsia brachycaulos 'Selecta'.

Tillandsia caput-medusae x Tillandsia brachycaulos. is a medium-sized hybrid. It is very easy to grow. When in bloom, it blushes a beautiful purple red.

Tillandsia edithae. In its habitat, It grows on rock and cliff. It is caulescent and looks white because the leaves are covered densely with scales. It grows well with bright light, and frequent watering. It grows very slowly and often take more than 10 years to bloom.

Tillanxsia schatzlii 'Red X'. A beautiful and easy to grow species. The succulent leaves are always pinkish purple. When in bloom, more colors are shown.

A beautiful form of Tillandsia brachycaulos.

TABLE OF CONTENTS

Tillandsia duratii is one of the most successful Tillandsia speceies. It grows well under a wide range of light, water and temperature conditions. Without roots, the curly leaves cling to its host like a monkey. The inflorescene of Tillandsia duratii develops for several months, and produces lovely lavender flowers that are heavily fragrant. 1

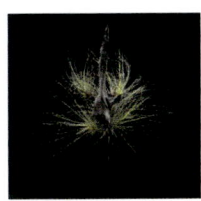

Tillandsia Juncifolia. The plant is easy to grow and always grow in large clumps. It flourishes when mounted in any position. 2

Tillandsia funckiana is a lovely plant and easy to grow, frequently grow many offsets along the stem and form a magnificent clump. It grows well in an airy, bright location. 3

Tillandsia funckiana growing in a clump. 4

Tillandsia ionantha v. vanhyningii. There are many forms of Tillandsia ionantha. It is the only form of ionantha that is caulescent. It has thick, succulent leaves and slow growing. It comes from one cliff in Mexico and is relatively rare.

5

Tillandsia velutina. This plant comes from Guatemala. It has a velvety look and feel. It likes plenty of water and bright location.

6

Tillandsia rodrigueziana x Tillandsia brachycaulos. The leaves of this beautiful hybrid are apple green, softer and thinner than the T. rodrigueziana. It is very easy to grow.

7

Tillandsia rodrigueziana x Tillandsia brachyculos growing on an old coconut.

8

Tillandsia harrisii. This is a very attractive and extremely hardy species. The thick soft leaves have a velvety surface. The plant produces a single pinkish to red inflorescence with tubular purple flowers.

9

Bathing in the sunny rain. Tillandsias are found mainly in the tropical rainforest in the Latin America, so light, water and air circulation are the key factors for keeping healthy Tilladnsia.

10

Tillandsia bulbosa. A very attractive plant with long, twisting cylindrical bright-green leaves that grow from a bulbous base. When in bloom, it produces bracts that become bright red, from which emerge tubular purple flowers. It produces a few offsets around the base of the parent plant after flowering, and becoming a spectacular multi-plant specimen in time.   11

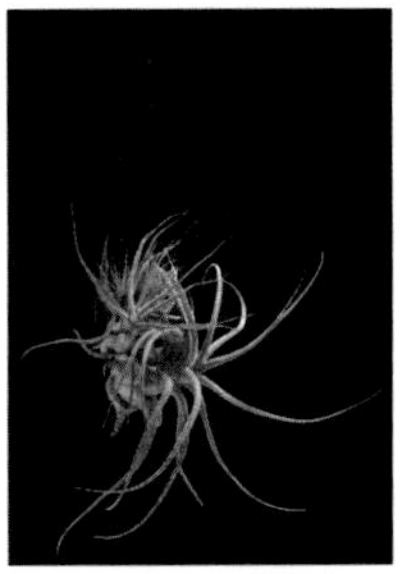

Tillandsia ehlersiana. It is one of the most interesting looking of all tillandsias.   12

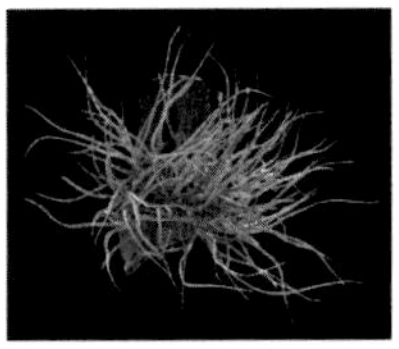

Tillandsia baileyi. It is a stemless species that always grow in dense clumps. It is easy to take care and can grow to quite large in good conditions.   13

Tillandsia funckiana x Tillandsia ionantha. This beautiful hybrid is easy to grow but slow growing.   14

Tillandsia pseudobaileyi. It has a frosted, silvery appearance as the plant is densely covered with trichomes. The leaves are furrowed longitudinally with thin amethyst lines.   15

A beautiful display of Tillandsia pseudobaiyi in the morning light.   16

Tillandsia filifolia is a popular species among collectors. The leaves are long, thin and green in colour, so it requires watering frequently in dry climates. It normally produces two or three offsets. Seedling grown from seeds needs some ten to twelve years to mature. 17

Tillandsia vernicosa. It is a hardy species, and the leaves are stiff and brittle. It looks very much like Tillandsia concolor but much smaller. The floral bracts are red and the flowers are white. 18

Tillandsia vernicosa. 19

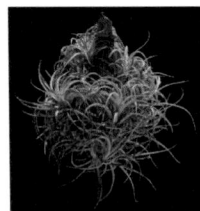

Tillandsia recurvifolia v. subsecundifolia. It is a hardy plants that requires bright light to thrive. It looks like T. harrisii but the leaves are curve and grow to one side. 20

Tillandsia ionantha 'Fuego'. Tillandsia ionantha is a popular species and is always the first Tillandsia one acquires. It is attractive, small and easy to cultivate. The leaves always form a pretty rosette. It often grows in clumps. When in bloom, the leaves of most ionantha flush to red, with tubular purple flowers. There are many forms of Tillandsia ionantha. Plants from different areas have different forms, sizes, shapes and colors. 21

Tillandsia ionantha 'Rosita'. 22

Tillandsia ionantha 'Guat'. 23

A small form of Tillandsia ionantha. 24

A few forms of Tillandsia ionantha growing on a piece of drift wood. 25

A beautiful display of Tillandsia filifolia and Tillandsia ionantha growing together on a piece of drift wood. 26

The graceful form of Tillsndsia filifolia and the dwarf form of Tillandsia ionantha match perfectly. 27

Tillandsias can grow on trees, rocks and cliffs, not in soil. Without roots, they can also survive. So we can use them to create Tillandsia bonsai. 28

A small bonsai growing on a piece of rock. 29

Tillandsia bonsai. 30

Tillandsia bonsai. 31

Tillandsia bonsai. 32

A few species of Tillandsia growing on a jar to create this bonsai. 33

Landscape bonsai. 34

Tillandsia bonsai. 35

A few small plants growing on the stem of a tall plant. 36

Tillandsia bonsai. 37

Tillandsia bonsai. 38

Tillandsia bonsai. 39

Tillandsia bonsai. 40

Tillandsia bonsai. 41

 Tillandsia bonsai. 42

 Tillandsia bonsai. 43

 Tillandsia bonsai. 44

 Tillandsia bonsai. 45

 Tillandsia bonsai. 46

 Tillandsia bonsai. 47

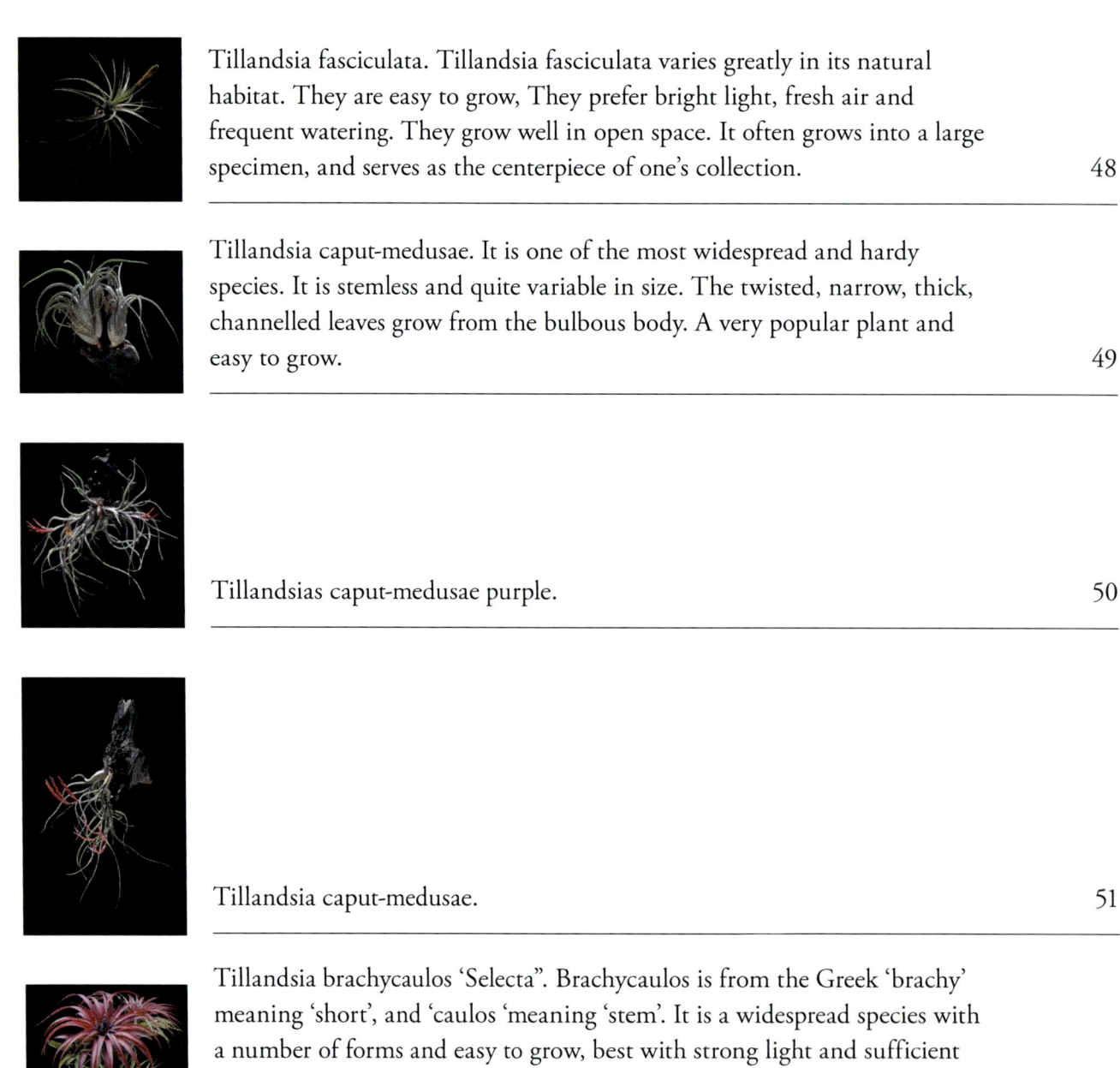

Tillandsia fasciculata. Tillandsia fasciculata varies greatly in its natural habitat. They are easy to grow, They prefer bright light, fresh air and frequent watering. They grow well in open space. It often grows into a large specimen, and serves as the centerpiece of one's collection. 48

Tillandsia caput-medusae. It is one of the most widespread and hardy species. It is stemless and quite variable in size. The twisted, narrow, thick, channelled leaves grow from the bulbous body. A very popular plant and easy to grow. 49

Tillandsias caput-medusae purple. 50

Tillandsia caput-medusae. 51

Tillandsia brachycaulos 'Selecta". Brachycaulos is from the Greek 'brachy' meaning 'short', and 'caulos 'meaning 'stem'. It is a widespread species with a number of forms and easy to grow, best with strong light and sufficient watering. Tillandsia beachycaulos 'Selecta' has apple-green leaves that turn ruby red when in bloom. 52

Another form a fasiculata. 53

Tillandsia reichenbachii. It looks like a small Tillandsia duratii. It rarely grows more than 16 cm. across and 10 cm.tall. The flowers are fragrant and have three different colors, deep purple, light purple and white. 54

Tillandsia brachycaulos "Selecta.Brachycaulos is from the Greek brachy,meaning 'short', and caulos, meaning 'stem'. It id s widespread species with a number of forms. It is easy to grow, best with strong light and sufficient watering. Tillandsia brachycaulos 'Selecta' has apple-green leaves that turn ruby red when in bloom. 55

Tillandsia brachycaulos 'Selecta'. 56

Tillandsia caput-medusae x Tillandsia brachycaulos. is a medium-sized hybrid. It is very easy to grow. When in bloom, it blushes a beautiful purple red. 57

Tillandsia edithae. In its habitat, It grows on rock and cliff. It is caulescent and looks white because the leaves are covered densely with scales. It grows well with bright light, and frequent watering. It grows very slowly and often take more than 10 years to bloom. 58

Tillanxsia schatzlii 'Red X'. A beautiful and easy to grow species. The succulent leaves are always pinkish purple. When in bloom, more colors are shown. 59

A beautiful form of Tillandsia brachycaulos. 60

Made in the USA
Coppell, TX
11 April 2025